31472400399691

D0712951

123 SESAME STREET

WELCOMING WORDS

WELCOME TO ARABIC
with SESAME STREET

J. P. PRESS

Lerner Publications ◆ Minneapolis

Dear Parents and Educators,

From its very beginning, *Sesame Street* has promoted mutual respect and cultural understanding by featuring a cast of diverse and lovable characters. *Welcome to Arabic* introduces children to the wonderful, wide world we live in. In this book *Sesame Street* friends present handy and fun vocabulary in a language kids may not know. These words can help young readers welcome new friends. Have fun as you explore!

Sincerely,

The Editors at Sesame Workshop

Table of Contents

WELCOME!

أهلاً بك!

Say ah-LAAN-bika

How to Speak Arabic

Did you know that the Arabic alphabet uses different letters? You read it from right to left. Practice speaking Arabic! Each word is broken up into separate sounds called syllables. Do you see the syllable in CAPITAL LETTERS? That's the sound that you emphasize the most!

Hello.

مرحباً.

mar-HAB-aan

Meet No'man! He is from the United Arab Emirates (UAE).

What is your name?

ما اسمك؟

M-ism-UK

My name is . . .

اسمي . . .

is-MI . . .

friendship

صداقة

sa-DA-qa

Will you be my friend?

هل ستصبح صديقي؟

HAL-sa-TU-sbih-sa-dIqi

We are best
friends!

نحن أفضل أصدقاء!

Meet my family!

قابل عائلتي!

10

dad
أب
AB

mom
أم
UM

brother
أخ
AKH

sister
أخت
UKHT

grandma
جدة
JA-da

grandpa
جد
JAD

Thank you.
شكراً لك.
shkr-AAN-LA-ka

You are welcome.
عفواً.
af-WAN

Please.
رجاءً.
RA-ja

I'm sorry.
أنا آسف.
ANA-a-sif

breakfast
فطور
fvu-TOR

lunch
غداء
GHA-daa

dinner
عشاء
ash-aa

14

I'm thirsty.

أنا عطشان.

ana-at-SHAN

I'm hungry.

أنا جائع.

ANA-JA-yie

How are you?

كيف حالك؟

KAYF-HA-luk

I'm fine, thank you.

بخير، شكراً لك.

bi-KHAYR, shuk-RAAN-LA-ka

Meet Shams! She is from the UAE.

Elmo loves you.
Elmo تحبك.

17

happy
مسرور
mas-RUR

sad
حزين
ha-ZIN

18

proud

فخور

FA-khur

excited

مبتهج

mub-TA-hij

animals
حيوانات
hay-WA-nat

fish
سمكة
sa-MA-ka

bird
عصفور
es-FOR

cat
قطة
qi-TA

My favorite color is . . .

لوني المفضل . . .

LA-wni-al-MU-fadal . . .

colors

ألوان

al-WAN

red
أحمر
ah-MAR

orange
برتقالي
burto-QA-li

yellow
أصفر
as-FAR

green
أخضر
akh-DAR

blue
أزرق
az-RAQ

purple
بنفسجي
ba-NA-fsaji

toys

ألعاب

al-AAB

jump

يقفز

YA-qfiz

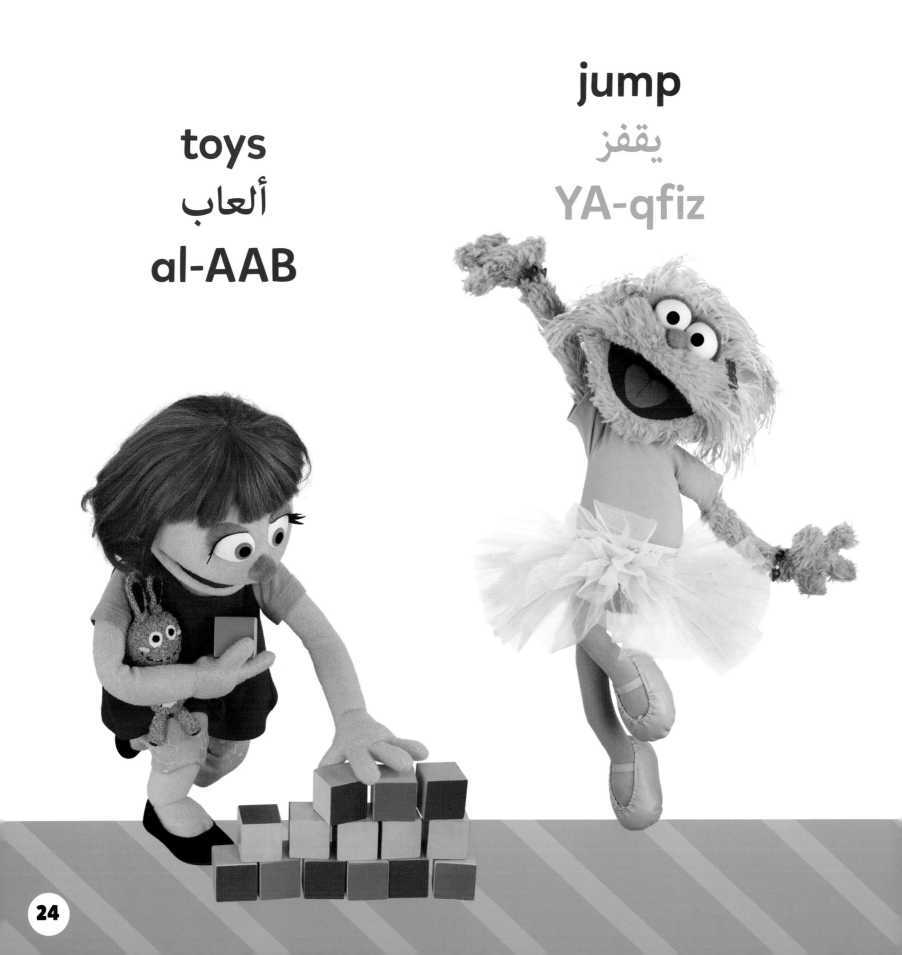

24

What do you like to do?
ماذا تحب أن تعمل؟

MA-dha-tuhi-BU-AN-te-MAL

We like to play!
نحب أن نلعب!

Goodbye.

وداعاً.

wa-DA-an

See you soon!

أراك قريباً!

ar-AAK-qary-BAAN

Count It!

1 one
واحد
WA-hid

2 two
اثنان
eth-NAN

3 three
ثلاثة
tha-LA-tha

4 four
أربعة
ar-BA-a

5 five
خمسة
kham-SA

6 six
ستة
si-TA

7 seven
سبعة
sab-AA

8 eight
ثمانية
tha-MA-nia

9 nine
تسعة
tis-AA

10 ten
عشرة
ash-aa-RA

Elmo's Favorite Words

That tickles!

ذلك يضحك!

tha-li-KA-YU-dhik

Welcome to my home.

أهلاً بك في منزلي.

ahl-AAN-bi-KA-FI-MA-nzi-li

Elmo is happy to see you!

Elmo مسرور برؤيتك!

El-MO-masr-UR-biru-a-YA-tik

Further Information

Sesame Street: Whoopi Goldberg and Elmo Draw Picture for Pen Pal in Syria
https://www.youtube.com/watch?v=fNJ51FvQ4NI

Billings, Patricia. *My First Bilingual Book—Friends (English-Arabic)*. Chicago: Milet, 2018.

Hello-World: Arabic
http://www.hello-world.com/languages.php/?language=Arabic

My First Bilingual Book—Fruit (English-Arabic). Chicago: Milet, 2016.

Sesame Street
http://www.sesamestreet.org

Lerner Publications Company
An imprint of Lerner Publishing Group, Inc.
241 First Avenue North
Minneapolis, MN 55401 USA

For reading levels and more information, look up this title at www.lernerbooks.com.

Main body text set in Mikado.
Typeface provided by HVD.

Additional image credits: clarst5/Shutterstock.com, p. 20 (bird); Eric Isselee/Shutterstock.com, p. 20 (cat); Gunnar Pippel/Shutterstock.com, p. 20 (fish); Super Prin/Shutterstock.com, p. 23 (butterfly); Viktar Malyshchyts/Shutterstock.com, pp. 28, 29 (orange).

Library of Congress Cataloging-in-Publication Data

Names: Press, J. P., 1993– author. | Children's Television Workshop, contributor.
Title: Welcome to Arabic with Sesame Street / J. P. Press.
Other titles: Sesame Street (Television program)
Description: Minneapolis, MN : Lerner Publications, 2019. | Series: Sesame Street welcoming words | Includes bibliographical references.
Identifiers: LCCN 2018059349 (print) | LCCN 2019009699 (ebook) | ISBN 9781541562479 (eb pdf) | ISBN 9781541555020 (lb : alk. paper) | ISBN 9781541574922 (pb : alk. paper)
Subjects: LCSH: Arabic language—Conversation and phrase books—English—Juvenile literature.
Classification: LCC PJ6309 (ebook) | LCC PJ6309 .P74 2019 (print) | DDC 492.7/83421—dc23

LC record available at https://lccn.loc.gov/2018059349

Manufactured in the United States of America
1-45827-42704-3/11/2019